WALES

Alice Harman

WAYLAND

FACT CAT

Get your paws on this fantastic new mega-series from Wayland!

Join our Fact Cat on a journey of fun learning about every subject under the sun!

First published in 2014 by Wayland
© Wayland 2014

Wayland
Hachette Children's Books
338 Euston Road
London NW1 3BH

Wayland Australia
Level 17/207 Kent Street
Sydney NSW 2000

Produced for Wayland by
White-Thomson Publishing Ltd
www.wtpub.co.uk
+44 (0) 843 208 7460

Editor: Alice Harman
Design: Rocket Design (East Anglia) Ltd
Fact Cat illustrations: Shutterstock/Julien Troneur
Other illustrations: Stefan Chabluk
Consultant: Kate Ruttle

A catalogue for this title is available from the British Library

ISBN: 978 0 7502 8438 7
ebook ISBN: 978 0 7502 8734 0

Dewey Number: 914.2 '9-dc23

10 9 8 7 6 5 4 3 2 1

Wayland is a division of Hachette Children's Books,
an Hachette UK company.
www.hachette.co.uk

Printed and bound in China

Picture and illustration credits:
Alamy: Rick Strange cover, travelib wales 6, aberCPC 9, George S de Blonsky 17; Chabluk, Stefan: 4; Dreamstime: Lukasz Kielas 5, Acceleratorhams 7, Thierry Maffeis 10, Gerald Marella 15; National Showcaves Centre: 19; Shutterstock: JuliusKielaltis 1 & 11, Jane Rix 8, Robyn McKenzie 13, Maxisport 16, Gail Johnson 18, nazlisart cover flag; Superstock: Food and Drink 12; Thinkstock: MikeLane45 14 & 22; Wikimedia: 20.

Every effort has been made to clear copyright. Should there be any inadvertent omission, please apply to the publisher for rectification.

The author, Alice Harman, is a writer and editor specialising in children's educational publishing.

The consultant, Kate Ruttle, is a literacy expert and SENCO, and teaches in Suffolk.

FACT CAT FACT

There is a question for you to answer on each spread in this book. You can check your answers on page 24.

CONTENTS

WELCOME TO WALES

Wales is part of the United Kingdom, which is often called the UK. England, Scotland and Northern Ireland are also part of the UK.

People in Wales often speak both English and Welsh. Can you find out how to say 'Good morning' in Welsh?

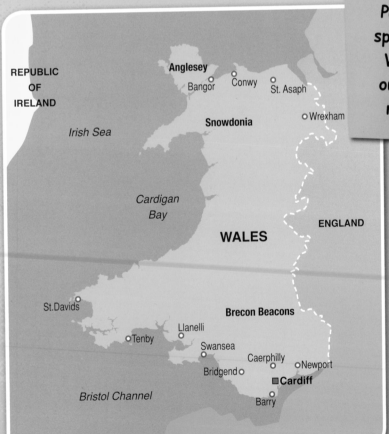

REPUBLIC OF IRELAND

Anglesey
Bangor Conwy St. Asaph
Wrexham

Irish Sea

Snowdonia

Cardigan Bay

WALES ENGLAND

St.Davids

Brecon Beacons

Llanelli
Tenby Swansea
Caerphilly Newport
Bridgend
Cardiff

Bristol Channel Barry

United Kingdom

EUROPE

4

Cardiff is the **capital** city of Wales. Around 350,000 people live there, and more than 18 million **tourists** visit the city every year. It has a famous castle and the Millennium Stadium.

Cardiff Bay is a lively area of the city where people can learn about history, play sports and go shopping.

FACT CAT FACT

Until around 150 years ago, Cardiff was a small town. Then large **coalmines** were dug in other parts of Wales, and the coal was sent to Cardiff. The city grew as many workers came to help **ship** the coal to other countries.

CITIES AND TOWNS

The three biggest cities in Wales are Cardiff, Swansea and Newport. They are all on the south coast. People who live there can sail boats on the sea.

This picture of Swansea was taken from the Meridian Tower, the tallest building in Wales. Can you find out how tall this tower is?

Bangor, St Davids and St Asaph are small Welsh cities. Some of the biggest towns in Wales are Wrexham, Bridgend, Llanelli, Caerphilly and Barry.

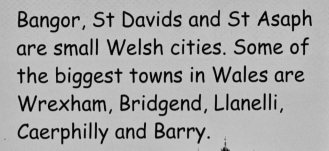

St Davids is the UK's smallest city. Around 1600 people live there. It has a large **cathedral** that is more than 800 years old.

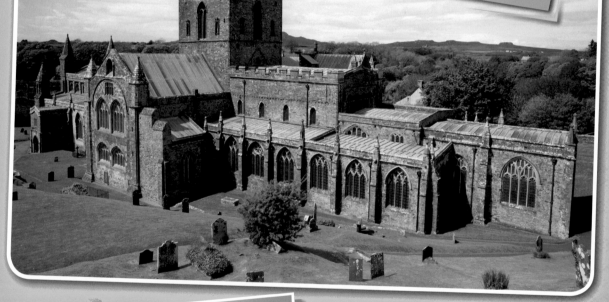

FACT CAT FACT

A small town in Wales has the longest place name in the world. It is called Llanfairpwllgwyngyllgogerychwyrndrobwyll-llantysiliogogogoch.

COUNTRYSIDE

Wales has lots of high mountains and hills. Many of them are in the famous areas of Snowdonia and the Brecon Beacons. People enjoy walking and climbing to see the beautiful views.

Mount Snowdon is the highest mountain in Wales. People can walk or take a train up to the top. Can you find out if it is the tallest mountain in the UK?

Most of the land in Wales is countryside. However, the soil in many areas is not good for growing **crops**. Most Welsh farmers keep animals such as sheep, cows, pigs, chickens and goats.

Sheep are the most common farm animals in Wales. Farmers cut their thick coats in the summer. The **wool** can be used to make clothes.

FACT CAT FACT

There are more than 6 million sheep in Wales. Just over 3 million people live in Wales. This means Wales has twice as many sheep as people!

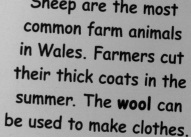

THE COAST

Wales has a long, beautiful coastline. There are tall **cliffs** and sandy beaches. Many Welsh towns and cities are on the coast.

Rhossili Bay has been **voted** one of the world's most beautiful beaches. Tourists like to visit it in the summer.

Wales has 50 **islands** off its coast. The largest island is called Anglesey, and around 70,000 people live there. Other islands are very small, and nobody lives on them.

South Stack is a very small island near to Anglesey. It has a tall, famous lighthouse. Can you find out what lighthouses are used for?

FACT CAT FACT

Skomer Island is known for its many wild animals and plants. However, there are no trees on the island. They were all cut down thousands of years ago, and no more ever grew.

FOOD

Welsh dishes often include meat, cheese and vegetables such as potatoes, carrots and **leeks**. People on the coast also eat a lot of fish and **shellfish**.

Cawl is a stew made with meat and vegetables. People in Wales have cooked cawl for more than 700 years.

Many **traditional** Welsh foods are popular today. Laverbread cakes are made from **seaweed** and **oatmeal**. Welsh rarebit is a special type of cheese on toast, made with egg and spices.

Today, some people eat Welsh rarebit with tomatoes. Try to find a recipe for Welsh rarebit, and ask an adult to help you make it.

FACT CAT FACT

Welsh rarebit used to be called 'Welsh rabbit', although it has never been made with rabbit! One story says that it had this name because a poor man couldn't catch a rabbit, and so had to make cheese on toast instead.

WILDLIFE

Wales has lots of **nature reserves** where wild animals can live safely. There are **rare** birds, butterflies and other animals in different areas around the country.

Polecats almost died out in the UK around 100 years ago. Today, there are around 17,000 of them living in Wales.

Many different sea animals live around the coast of Wales. People take boat trips to see sharks, seals, sea turtles, dolphins, **porpoises** and whales.

There are more than 250 bottlenose dolphins living around Cardigan Bay. Can you find out where else in the world this type of dolphin lives?

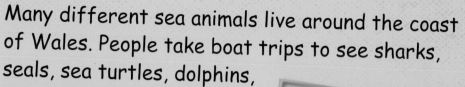

FACT CAT FACT

The largest ever sea turtle was found on the coast of Wales around 25 years ago. It was almost 3 metres (9 feet) long, and weighed over 900 kg (2000 lbs). It was around 100 years old.

15

SPORT

Rugby is the most popular sport in Wales. There are more than 230 rugby clubs across the country. Many people also enjoy watching and playing football.

Gareth Bale is a famous Welsh football player. He was only 16 years old when he first played for Wales.

Tanni Grey-Thompson has won 11 gold **Paralympic** medals for wheelchair racing. Can you find out how many silver medals she has won?

Other sports such as **athletics**, basketball, cycling and **snooker** are also popular in Wales. There are lots of famous Welsh sportspeople who take part in **international** competitions.

FACT CAT FACT

Colin Jackson is one of the fastest **hurdling** racers of all time. Between 1993 and 1995, Colin Jackson raced 44 times without losing a single race.

17

SIGHTS

Tourists come from all over the world to see Welsh castles. There used to be more than 400 castles across the country. Today, around 100 are still standing.

Conwy Castle was built more than 700 years ago. It is one of the most visited castles because it is so large and well **preserved**.

The National Showcaves Centre is one of the most popular places to visit. It has 17 km (11 miles) of underground caves. Some of them have streams and waterfalls.

The Cathedral Cave is one of the three caves that visitors can walk through. Can you find out the names of the other two?

FAMOUS PEOPLE

George Everest and Henry Morton Stanley are famous Welsh explorers. Mount Everest, the highest mountain in the world, is named after George Everest.

Stanley travelled around an area of Africa called the Congo. He also found a missing explorer. Can you find out what that explorer's name was?

FACT CAT FACT

When Stanley was six years old, he was sent to live at a **workhouse**. His father had died, and his family could not look after him. He lived at the workhouse until he was 15 years old.

Many popular actors, musicians and writers come from Wales. The famous children's author Roald Dahl grew up in Wales. He wrote *Charlie and the Chocolate Factory*, *Matilda* and many other books.

Charlotte Church became a famous **classical** singer when she was only 11 years old. She is now a pop singer and TV presenter.

QUIZ

Try to answer the questions below. Look back through the book to help you. Check your answers on page 24.

1 How many islands are there off the coast of Wales?

a) 10
b) 50
c) 75

2 Which sport is Gareth Bale famous for playing?

a) football
b) rugby
c) basketball

3 St David's is the biggest city in the UK. True or not true?

a) true
b) not true

4 Which Welsh animal is shown in the picture below?

a) porpoise
b) seal
c) polecat

5 Welsh rarebit is made with seaweed. True or not true?

a) true
b) not true

GLOSSARY

athletics sport that includes different running races and other jumping and throwing activities

capital the city where the government (the group of people that leads the country) meets

cathedral large, important church

classical music that was often written a long time ago, and is more serious than pop music

cliff high, steep wall of rock

coalmine hole made in the ground, from which coal is taken; coal is a hard, dark material that is burned for heat or energy

crops plants that are grown for food

hurdling type of running race in which people jump over barriers

international to do with two or more countries

island area of land completely surrounded by water

leek long, white and green vegetable

nature reserve area of land and/or sea where no one can damage the plants or animals living there

oatmeal dry food made from oats, which are seeds from a plant

Paralympics a famous worldwide sports competition for people who have disabilities

porpoise animal that lives in the sea and breathes air; it looks a lot like a dolphin

preserved kept in a good state, so that no damage is done

rare not found or seen very often

seaweed plant that grows in the sea

shellfish small animal that lives in water and has its body inside a hard shell

ship to carry something across water in a ship

snooker sport in which people use long sticks to hit hard balls into holes in the corners of a table

tourist person who visits a place for a holiday

traditional describes something that a group of people has done or made the same way for a long time

voted chosen by a group of people

wool thick, soft hair of sheep

workhouse building in which people worked for food and somewhere to sleep

INDEX

ANSWERS

Pages 4–20

Page 4: 'Bore da' means 'Good morning' in Welsh. It is pronounced 'bor eh dar'.

Page 6: The Meridian Tower is 107 m (351 ft) tall.

Page 8: No, Ben Nevis is the highest mountain in the UK. It is in Scotland. Mount Snowdon is 1085 m (3560 ft) tall, but Ben Nevis is 1344 m (4410 ft).

Page 11: Lighthouses are tall buildings that have a strong light at the top of them. At night or in bad weather, this light tells people on ships where the coast is so that they don't crash into the rocks.

Page 15: Bottlenose dolphins live almost all over the world! The only parts of the ocean where they are not found are the Arctic and Antarctic. These are the very cold areas in the north and south of the world.

Page 17: Tanni Grey-Thompson has won four silver Paralympic medals.

Page 19: The other two caves are called Dan-y-Ogof and Bone Cave.

Page 20: The missing explorer's name was Dr David Livingstone.

Quiz answers

1	b)	4	c)
2	a)	5	b)
3	b)		

OTHER TITLES IN THE FACT CAT SERIES...

SPACE

THE EARTH
978 0 7502 8220 8

THE MOON
978 0 7502 8221 5

THE PLANETS
978 0 7502 8222 2

THE SUN
978 0 7502 8223 9

COUNTRIES

FRANCE
978 0 7502 8212 3

BRAZIL
978 0 7502 8213 0

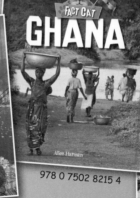
GHANA
978 0 7502 8215 4

ITALY
978 0 7502 8214 7

WAYLAND